Nita Mehta's
THAI Vegetarian Cookery

Vegetarian

100% TRIED & TESTED RECIPES

Nita Mehta
B.Sc. (Home Science), M.Sc. (Food and Nutrition) Gold Medalist

Tanya Mehta

SNAB
PUBLISHERS PVT LTD

Nita Mehta's

T H A I Vegetarian Cookery

© Copyright 2004 **SNAB** Publishers Pvt Ltd

First Edition 2004
ISBN 81-7869-082-9

Food Styling and Photography: **SNAB**

Layout and laser typesetting :

National Information
Technology Academy
3A/3, Asaf Ali Road
New Delhi-110002
☎ 23252948

Published by :

Publishers Pvt. Ltd.
3A/3 Asaf Ali Road,
New Delhi - 110002
Tel: 23252948, 23250091
Telefax:91-11-23250091

Editorial and Marketing office:
E-159, Greater Kailash-II, N.Delhi-48
Fax: 91-11-29225218, 29229558
Tel: 91-11-29214011, 29218727, 29218574
E-Mail: nitamehta@email.com
snab@snabindia.com
*Website:*http://www.nitamehta.com
Website: http://www.snabindia.com

Distributed by :
THE VARIETY BOOK DEPOT
A.V.G. Bhavan, M 3 Con Circus,
New Delhi - 110 001
Tel : 23417175, 23412567; Fax : 23415335
Email: varietybookdepot@rediffmail.com

Printed by :
AJANTA OFFSET & PACKAGING LTD

Rs. 89/-

Introduction

*I*n Thailand, food is a celebration. For a Thai, cooking is a source of pride. Thai food is a combination of delicious aroma, brilliant colours and exotic spices. Thai cooking is simple, quick and healthy. It is particularly appealing because of its healthy, low fat method of cooking.

Thai cuisine is a confluence of Chinese, Malaya and Indian influence, which the Thai have skilfully adapted as distinctly their own. Try a traditional satay with peanut sauce, followed by red Thai curry and crispy vegetables with a tangy dipping sauce. Accompany these with Masaman Curried Rice or with Glass Noodles in sesame paste. Finish the meal with a wonderful dessert- Crispy Fried Ice-Cream ball.

All the ingredients used in the recipes are easily available although their substitutes have been given in case of non-availability.

Discover the secrets of Thai cooking with this beautiful illustrated book. Follow the step by step instruction to make classic Thai meals in your own home.

Happy cooking!

Nita Mehta

About The Recipes

What's In A Cup?

INDIAN CUP
1 teacup = 200 ml liquid
AMERICAN CUP
1 cup = 240 ml liquid (8 oz.)
The recipes in this book were tested with the Indian teacup which holds 200 ml liquid.

CONTENTS

SALADS   33

SNACKS WITH DIPS   44

VEGETABLE CURRIES   60

Ingredients used in Thai food

Basil : It belongs to the 'tulsi' family. It is available in dried form or as fresh basil leaves which are packed and sold by some vegetable vendors. Dried form is also available, substitute 2 tsp of dried for ¼ cup of fresh leaves. Tulsi leaves (Holy basil) can be substituted for basil. To store basil, keep standing basil in a glass of water with the leaves above the water. It keeps them fresh & green for a few days. During winters, keep it outside & in summers keep basil in the glass in the fridge. Basil seeds grow into beautiful plants if put into a pot.

Lemon grass : The flavour of lemon grass is similar to that of lemon, yet it has its very own unique taste. To use, discard the bottom 1" of the stalk and peel some of the outer leaves. Chop the stalk and use it in curry pastes. The upper grass like portion is not edible, so it is added to dishes like soups, rice and curries to flavour them but  removed from the dish before serving. Lemon grass will keep well for about 1-2 weeks in the fridge. Use 1-2 stalks per dish.

Black Bean Sauce: This sauce is made from fermented black beans. It has a pungent and salty flavour. It cannot be made at home. It is available ready-made in bottles, at most leading stores (shops).

Lemon Rind: In absence of lemon grass, lemon rind makes a good substitute. To get lemon rind, grate a firm, fresh lemon on the finest holes of the grater without applying pressure. Grate only the yellow outer skin without grating the white pith beneath it. Rind of 2 lemons would do good for a stalk of lemon grass.

 **Seasoning Cube & Veg Stock:** Veg stock is an important agent for most soup and sauces. However, if you do not have stock ready or feel lazy to make a stock, you can use seasoning cubes mixed in water instead. Seasoning cubes are available as small packets. These are very salty, so taste the dish after adding the cube before you put more salt. Always crush the seasoning cube to a powder before using it.

Five Spice Powder: This mixture of five ground spices is slightly sweet and pungent. Roast together 2 tsp peppercorns (saboot kali mirch), 3 star anise (phool chakri), 6 cloves (laung), 4" stick cinnamon (dalchini), 3 tsp fennel (saunf). Grind all the ingredients of the powder in a small mixer to a powder. Strain the powder through a sieve (channi).

Soya Sauce: There are 2 kinds. One is dark and the other is light. Both are used for seasoning all foods. It cannot be made at home. It is available ready made in bottles, at most leading stores (shops).

Kaffir lime leaves (nimbu ke patte): These have a distinctive flavour and perfume. The leaves are available dried, frozen or fresh from Oriental food shops and some greengrocers. If kaffir lime leaves are unavailable, any leaves of an Indian lemon tree or a plant would do. In this book we have not specified the use of kaffir limes for lime juice, but for a true Thai flavour use it whenever possible.

Coconut cream and milk: It is the liquid extracted from coconut flesh. Coconut cream is the liquid extracted from the first pressing. Coconut cream is the thickest and most concentrated extract. Coconut milk is the product of the second and third pressing and is much thinner.

Coconut milk is used in curries, while coconut cream is used mainly in desserts. Coconut cream is available in tetra packs or cans and can be diluted with water to make coconut milk. Coconut milk powder which is available can be mixed with some water to make coconut milk. The recipe at the end of this book is very easy to follow.

Star Anise *(Chakri Phool)*: The dried, hard, brown, star shaped fruit has a fennel flavour. It is an important ingredient used in five spice powder. It can be substituted with saunf (fennel seeds).

Noodles: Thin noodles are preferred to thick ones. They are usually cooked in boiling water till just done for about 1 minute only. Never overcook noodles as they turn thick on over cooking. They are cooked to a crisp tender stage.

Rice Noodles: These thin noodles resemble long, transculent white hair. They are just soaked in hot water for 10 minutes and then drained before use. When deep fried they explode dramatically into a tangle of airy, crunchy strands that are used for garnish. The thin noodles are called **glass noodles**. In the absence of these, regular noodles or rice seviyaan can be used.

Flat Noodles: These are also rice noodles, the only difference being they are flatter and wider to look. In absence of these, use flat pasta (fettucine).

White glutinous rice/Sticky Rice: This rice can either be long or short grained For savoury dishes, Thai cooks would use the long grain variety. Glutinous rice is very high in starch content, the cooked grains cling together in a mass and are soft and sticky. Short grain white glutinous rice is mainly used for desserts. You can use any ordinary quality rice for this.

Rice flour: Ready-made rice flour is easily available in the market. To make it at home, grind raw rice (kachcha chaawal) to a smooth powder. Sift through a sieve (channi) to get a fine powder.

Bean Sprouts: These are shoots of moong beans or soya beans. The texture is crisp. To make bean sprouts at home, soak ½ cup of green beans (saboot moong dal) for about 8 hours. Discard water & tie in a muslin cloth. Keep it tied for 2-3 days, remembering to wet the cloth each day. When shoots are long enough, wash carefully in water. Fresh bean sprouts will keep for 3-4 days if refrigerated in a plastic bag.

Simple Garnishes

Picture on page 19

Spring Onion Flowers: To make spring onion flowers, cut off about ¼ inch piece from the white bulb end and leaving 3" from the bulb, cut off the greens. Slice the bulb thinly lengthwise till the end of the bulb. Now make similar cuts at right angles. Similarly for a green side, cut the green leaves with a pair of scissors, almost till the stem end to get thin

strips. Place in iced water for some time until it opens up like a flower.

Chilli Flower: *A chilli flower made from fresh red or green chilli is a wonderful garnish for a spicy dish.*
Choose a slightly thick chilli. Cut into half starting from the tip almost till the end,  leaving ½" from the stem end. Cut each half with a scissor into many thin strips, keeping all intact at the base. Put the chilli in chilled water for 4-5 hours in the fridge. It opens up to a flower.

Mango Hedgehogs: Take a ripe, firm mango – avoid using the fibrous variety. Slice off two pieces from either side of the seed. Cut parallel lines with a knife, about ½" apart, along the length of the mango. Cut parallel lines at right angles to these, the same distance apart. You must go right down to the skin, but be extremely careful that you do not cut through the skin. Hold slice firmly & with the tips of your fingers, push it out from the back, carefully, applying pressure on the thickest part. The slice will open out to resemble a hedgehog, and will retain this shape. Use this as a  garnish to decorate fruit desserts. You can do the same with plums also.

Carrot & Radish Tuberoses:
These look great when placed on the side of a salad, or next to the snacks on the serving
platter. A sprig of green leaves of coriander, mint or parsley placed next to the flowers make them look prettier.

Take a slender carrot or radish. Peel and wash it. Make a sharp angled cut, at about a height of 1½", about ½" downwards and inwards. Make 2 similar cuts from the remaining sides - all the cuts should meet at the end. Hold the top of the carrot with one hand, and the base with the other. Twist the lower portion to break off the top portion. You will have a tuberose in one hand and the remaining part of the carrot in the other. Trim the left over carrot to get a pointed end. Make more flowers from the left over carrot. Keep them in ice-cold water for upto 3-4 days without getting spoilt. You can make such flowers with white radish (mooli) also.

 **Coloured Capsicum Baskets:** Slice the top of a coloured (yellow, red or green capsicum). Make ½" deep V cuts all around the edge to get a 'VVVV' edge. Leave the bunch of seeds in it as they are. Place on the side of a large platter of salad.

Curry Pastes

Although ready-made pastes are now readily available in jars and packets, but they are nothing in taste compared to the home made pastes prepared with fresh ingredients. And ofcourse, they are simple and quick to make in a mixer. You can make these curry pastes well in advance and store them in the fridge for 7-8 days. Use them whenever required.

Red Curry Paste

Gives 1 cup

6-7 dry, red chillies, (preferably the broad Kashmiri variety as it imparts a bright red colour) - break red chillies into two, discard seeds, soak in ¼ cup warm water for 10 minutes
½ onion - chopped, 8-10 flakes garlic - peeled, ½" piece ginger - sliced
1 stick lemon grass - the lower stem is cut into small pieces, discard the leaves or rind of 1 lemon (see page 11), ½ tsp peppercorns (saboot kali mirch), 1 tsp salt, ¼ tsp haldi
1 tbsp coriander seeds (saboot dhania), 1 tsp cumin seeds (jeera), 1 tbsp lemon juice

1. On a tawa, dry roast cumin and coriander seeds on low heat for about 2 minutes till they become aromatic and get roasted but not brown.
2. Put all the other ingredients and roasted seeds in a grinder and churn alongwith the water of the chillies to a smooth paste. Use as required. Store in a glass jar in the fridge.

¥ ¥ ¥ ¥ ¥ ¥
¥
¥
¥
¥

Green Curry Paste

Gives 1 cup (approx).

6-7 green chillies - deseeded and chopped
½ onion - chopped
1 tbsp chopped garlic, ½" piece ginger - chopped
1 stick lemon grass (use only the lower portion) - cut into pieces, discard the
leaves or rind of 1 lemon (see page 11)
2-3 lemon leaves (nimbu ke patte)
½ cup chopped coriander leaves or 1 cup fresh basil leaves
½ tsp salt, 15 peppercorns (saboot kali mirch)
1 tbsp lemon juice, ¼ tsp haldi
1 tbsp coriander seeds (saboot dhania), 1 tsp cumin seeds (jeera)

1. On a tawa, dry roast cumin and coriander seeds on low heat for about
    2 minutes till they become aromatic and get roasted but not brown.
2. Put all other ingredients of the curry paste and the roasted seeds in a
    grinder and grind to a fine paste, using a little water if required.
3. Use as required. Store in a glass jar in the fridge. Can be stored for 1
    week.   ***Thai Garnishes : on page 14*** ➢

Thai Garnishes

Mango Hedge Hogs

Carrot & Radish Tuberoses

Spring Onion Flower

Capsicum Basket

Chilli Flower

Yellow Curry Paste

Serves 5- 6

3 tsp turmeric powder (haldi)
1 stick lemon grass (use only the lower portion) - cut into pieces, discard the
leaves or rind of 1 lemon (see page 10, 11)
3 tbsp chopped fresh yellow or red chilli or 6 dried red chillies
½ onion or 2 shallots - finely chopped
8-10 flakes garlic - peeled, 1½" piece ginger or galangal - thinly sliced
1½ tsp coriander seeds (dhania saboot), 1 tbsp lemon juice
2 tsp five spice powder (see page 11)
1 tsp salt, ¼ tsp peppercorns (saboot kali mirch)
1 phool chakri (star anise) or 1 tsp saunf (fennel seeds)
2 laung (cloves), 1" stick dalchini (cinnamon)

1. Put all ingredients of curry paste in a kadhai and dry roast for about 3-4 minutes.
2. Grind all the roasted ingredients to a paste alongwith 4 tbsp water. Use as required or store in a glass jar in the fridge. Can be stored for 1 week.

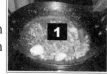

◅ *Green Mango 'n' Cashew Salad : Recipe on page 34*

Masaman Curry Paste

Serves 4

10 dried, red chillies, rind of 1 lemon (see page 11)
2 medium sized onions - chopped
12-14 flakes of garlic, 4 tsp chopped ginger
2 tbsp cumin seeds (jeera), 2 tsp saunf (fennel seeds)
2" stick dalchini (cinnamon), seeds of 4 moti illaichi (brown cardamom)
4 laung (cloves), 8 saboot kali mirch (black peppercorns)
4 tbsp saboot dhania (coriander seeds)
¼ tsp grated jaiphal (nutmeg)

1. For the paste, roast all ingredients of the paste in a kadhai/wok for 5 minutes or till fragrant. See picture.
2. Grind all the roasted ingredients to a paste alongwith 4 tbsp water. Use as required or store in a glass jar in the fridge. Can be stored for 1 week.

Soups

¥ ¥ ¥ ¥ ¥ ¥
¥
¥
¥
¥
¥

Lemon Coriander Soup

Picture on page 1   *Serves 4*

CLEAR STOCK
6 cups water
1 stick lemon grass - chopped or rind of 1 lemon (1 tsp rind)
¼ cup chopped coriander alongwith stalks
1" piece of ginger - washed, sliced without peeling
2 laung (cloves), 1 tej patta (bay leaf)
2 seasoning cubes (maggi or knorr or any other brand)

OTHER INGREDIENTS
1 tbsp oil, ¼ tsp red chilli flakes
½ carrot- - cut into paper thin slices, 2 mushrooms - cut into paper thin slices
2 baby corns - cut into paper thin slices, 1 tsp salt & ¼ tsp pepper or to taste
2 tbsp lemon juice, 1 tsp sugar, or to taste
2 tbsp cornflour dissolved in ¼ cup water
2 tbsp coriander leaves - torn roughly with the hands

1. If using lemon rind, wash and grate 1 lemon with the peel gently on
   the finest side of the grater to get lemon rind. Do not apply pressure
   and see that the white pith beneath the lemon peel is not grated along

with the yellow rind. The white pith is bitter!

2. Cut mushrooms into thin slices.
3. Cut carrot into paper thin slices diagonally (¼ cup).

4. For stock, mix all ingredients given under clear stock with 6 cups of water. Bring to a boil. Keep on low flame for 5 minutes. Strain the stock. If there is lemon grass, pick up most of the pieces and put back in the stock. Keep aside.
5. Heat 1 tsp oil in a wok. Remove from fire. Add ¼ tsp red chilli flakes.

6. Immediately, add carrot, mushrooms and baby corns cut into paper thin slices. Return to fire. Add pepper. Saute for 1 minute on medium flame.
7. Add the prepared stock into the vegetables in the wok. Boil. Add 1 tsp salt and sugar.

8. Add 2 tbsp cornflour dissolved in ¼ cup water, stirring continuously. Boil.
9. Add lemon juice & coriander leaves. Simmer for 1-2 minutes. Check salt, sugar and lemon juice. Add more if required. Remove from fire.
10. Add a few more green coriander leaves. Serve hot in soup bowls.

¥ ¥ ¥ ¥ ¥ ¥
¥
¥
¥
¥

Orient Noodle Soup

A spicy, hot, clear soup with lots of vegetables for the winter months. Lemon rind and tomato puree add a delicious flavour to this appetizer soup. Noodles make it different.

Picture on backcover   *Serves 4*

1½ tbsp oil
3 flakes garlic - chopped & crushed
4 mushrooms - sliced and then cut into thin long pieces
1 small carrot - grated, ½ capsicum - finely chopped
10-12 spinach leaves - shredded finely (cut into thin strips)
3 tbsp ready-made tomato puree
½ tsp red chilli flakes
30 gms noodles (½ cup) - break into 2" pieces
1¼ tsp salt, ¼ tsp pepper, 1 tsp sugar
rind of 1 lemon (1 tsp approx.), see step 1
2 tsp green chilli sauce
1 tsp vinegar
2 stock cubes - crushed

1. To take out lemon rind, grate a firm whole lemon on the finest holes of the grater without applying too much pressure. Grate only the upper yellow skin without grating the white bitter pith beneath the yellow skin. Keep rind aside.

2. Heat oil in a pan. Reduce heat and add garlic and red chilli flakes. Saute briefly for ½ minute.

3. Add mushrooms, carrot and capsicum. Stir fry for 1 minute.

4. Add tomato puree and red chillies. Stir for ½ minute.

5. Add 4 cups of water. Crush 2 stock cubes in it. Bring the soup to a boil. Add the noodles. Boil on medium heat for 2-3 minutes till noodles are soft.

6. Add salt, pepper, sugar, lemon rind, chilli sauce and vinegar.

7. Add the finely shredded spinach, simmer for 1 minute. Serve hot in soup bowls.

Tom Yum Pla

Thai hot and sour soup with vegetables and peanuts.

Picture on facing page   *Serves 3-4*

STOCK
1 cup chopped carrot, 1 onion - chopped
2 tbsp chopped celery stalks/coriander
1-2 sticks lemon grass - chopped
3-4 lemon leaves (nimbu ke patte)
1½ tsp black peppercorns (saboot kali mirch)

TO BE ADDED TO SOUP
1 medium/3 tbsp carrot - cut into 1" thin pieces
5 large / 100 gms fresh mushrooms - cut into thin, flat slices
3 tbsp bamboo shoots - cut into 1" long, thin pieces - optional
1 tbsp thin slices of ginger, 2 tbsp basil leaves
8-10 lemon leaves (nimbu ke patte), 1 tbsp lemon juice
¼ cup roasted peanuts (moongphali) - finely ground to a powder
½ tsp salt or to taste   *Contd...*

GRIND TO A PASTE
3 flakes garlic, 2 tbsp chopped coriander leaves
4-5 peppercorns (saboot kali mirch)

1. Put all the ingredients given under stock in a pressure cooker with 6 cups water.
2. Give 3-4 whistles. When the pressure drops, strain the soup without mashing the vegetables, so as to get a clear soup. Keep stock aside.
3. In a pan put 1 tbsp oil and fry the garlic-coriander-peppercorn paste for 1-2 minutes.
4. Add vegetables- carrots, mushrooms, bamboo shoots and ginger. Fry for 1-2 minutes.
5. Add basil and lemon leaves and the prepared stock.
6. Add lemon juice, peanut powder and salt to taste.
7. Let the soup simmer for 15-20 minutes. Serve hot garnished with coriander.

Note: If you like a thicker soup, add 1 tbsp cornflour mixed with ¼ cup water. Boil for 2-3 minutes on low flame after adding cornflour.

◁ *Spring Rolls : Recipe on page 48*

Tom Yum

Serves 4

3-4 kaffir lemon leaves (nimbu ke patte) - shredded
½ stalk lemon grass - cut into thin slices diagonally
2-3 mushrooms - cut into paper thin slices
½ small carrot - cut into paper thin diagonal slices
2 fresh red or green chillies - sliced diagonally and deseeded
1 tbsp coriander leaves, 2-3 tbsp lemon juice, 2 tsp of sugar
5 cups water, 2 stock cubes, 1-2 tsp light soya sauce
¾ tsp salt & ¼ tsp pepper, or to taste, 1 tbsp oil, ¼ cup coconut milk (optional)

RED CHILLI PASTE (CRUSH TOGETHER)

½ tsp red chilli flakes, 2-3 flakes garlic, ¾ tsp chopped ginger, ½ tsp salt

1. In a deep pan put 1 tbsp oil, add lemon leaves and lemon grass and the above red chilli paste. Mix well.
2. Add water. Crush stock cubes in it. Give one boil. Reduce heat and keep covered on low heat for 5 minutes.
3. Add mushrooms, carrots and fresh red chillies. Boil for 2 minutes.
4. Reduce heat. Add lemon juice, light soya sauce, salt, pepper and sugar to taste. Add coriander leaves. Simmer for 1 minute.
5. Add coconut milk. Remove from fire. Serve hot in soup bowls.

Salads

Green Mango 'n' Cashew Salad

A very unusual and quick salad. Goes well with an Indian meal too. It is generally eaten like a chutney, so make a small bowl for 4-6 people.

Picture on page 20   *Serves 6-8*

3 cups juliennes (match sticks) of raw green, mangoes (3 big mangoes)
½ cup roasted or fried kaju (cashew nuts) or peanuts
1-2 spring onions
OR
½ small onion and ½ capsicum - cut into shreds (thin long strips)
2-3 tbsp mango chutney (you can use home made or ready made)
1-2 dry red chillies - crushed (½ tsp)
1 tsp soya sauce
salt and pepper to taste
3-4 flakes garlic - crushed
1 tsp honey or powdered sugar if needed

1. Cut white bulb of spring onion into rings and greens into 1" diagonal pieces.
2. Peel green mangoes. Cut the side pieces. Cut into thin match sticks or juliennes. Keep aside.
3. Mix all ingredients except cashew nuts and honey in a bowl. Add sugar or honey if mangoes are very sour. Keep covered in the refrigerator for 2-3 hours for the flavour to penetrate.
4. At serving time, top with roasted or fried nuts and mix lightly.

Note: Ready-made mango chutney is available in the market in small bottles.

¥ ¥ ¥ ¥ ¥ ¥
¥
¥
¥
¥

Green Papaya Salad

The popular Thai salad with a chilli-lemon dressing. Choose a hard, raw papaya with a white flesh. Even a slightly ripe papaya with an orangish flesh is not suitable for this salad. Add light soya sauce, so that the salad is not discoloured.

Serves 4-6

3 cups grated hard, raw papaya (1 small kachcha papita), see note given below
1 tomato - cut into 4 pieces and deseeded, cut into small square pieces
½ cup tender green beans (French beans) - sliced very finely
¼ cup roasted peanuts (moongphali)- crushed coarsely

DRESSING
1 tsp light Soya sauce, 3 tbsp lemon juice
4 tbsp sugar syrup, or to taste - (see note)
½ tsp red chilli flakes, ½ tsp salt, or to taste

CRUSH TOGETHER
3-4 red or green chillies and 1 flake garlic

1. Crush together red or green chillies with garlic to a rough paste. Mix this paste with all the other ingredients of the dressing in a flat bowl.
2. Peel and grate papaya from medium holes into thick long shreds. Add chopped beans and tomatoes and papaya to the dressing in the flat dish. Mix well. Cover with a cling film and chill for at least one hour, so that the flavours penetrate.
3. To serve, mix in half the peanuts. Serve topped with rest of the roasted peanuts.

Note: For an authentic papaya salad, peel the papaya and cut into slices. Cut slices into juliennes (matchsticks). To make work simpler, I have grated the papaya. If using dark soya sauce, add just a few drops to keep the colour light.

Sugar syrup - boil ¼ cup sugar with ¼ cup water. Simmer for 1-2 minutes. Add according to your taste to Thai dishes.

Crunchy Salad with Rice Flakes

Picture on facing page   *Serves 4*

½ cup bean sprouts with long shoots
50 gms paneer- cut into ½" rectangular pieces
¼ cup roasted or fried kaju (cashew nuts)
1- 2 spring onions
½ red and ½ green capsicum - cut into shreds (thin long strips)
½ yellow capsicum - cut into 1" pieces

DRESSING

½ tbsp red chilli flakes, 1 tsp vinegar
1 tbsp soya sauce, ½ tsp salt and ½ tsp pepper or to taste
2 tbsp oil, 2 tbsp honey
1 tsp cumin (jeera), ½ tsp crushed garlic, 2 tbsp water

TOPPING

¼ cup raw rice (kachcha chaawal)

1. To prepare the topping, grind the raw rice to a rough powder in a mixer.
2. Heat a kadhai and put the rice flakes in it. Roast for 4-5 minutes. Keep aside.
3. Cut spring onion into rings till the greens.
4. Deep fry paneer pieces and cashewnuts till golden.
5. Mix all ingredients of the dressing in a small mixer (spice grinder). Churn well to make a paste.
6. Mix all the vegetables, paneer and half of roasted rice in a big bowl. Pour the prepared dressing over it, mix well and chill in the fridge till serving time.
7. At serving time, top with remaining half rice and fried nuts and mix lightly. Serve.

⊲ *Crispy Soft Corn : Recipe on page 54*
⊲ *Veg Satay with Peanut Sauce : Recipe on page 44*

¥ ¥ ¥ ¥ ¥ ¥
¥
¥
¥
¥

Glass Noodle Salad

Serves 6-8

3 cups glass noodles or rice vermicelli or thin white bean threads
8-10 french beans - cut into 1" diagonal pieces
100 gm baby corns - sliced diagonally thinly
1 large carrot
1 spring onion - chopped with greens (½ cup)

DRESSING

4 tbsp oil (sesame oil, preferably)
2 tbsp light soya sauce, use just a few drops if using a dark soya sauce
1 tbsp vinegar, 2 tbsp Worcestershire sauce
2 tbsp green chilli sauce, 2 tbsp red chilli sauce
2 tbsp tomato ketchup, 1 tsp crushed garlic
¾ tsp salt, ½ tsp pepper, 1 tsp sugar

TO GARNISH

1 tbsp roasted peanuts (moongphali) - split into two by rolling with a rolling pin
(chakla-belan)

1. To boil glass noodles, heat 4 cups of water in a pan with 1 tsp salt. Add noodles to boiling water. Remove from fire. Leave in hot water for 2 minutes or till noodles are slightly soft. Strain and refresh in cold water immediately. Let them be in the strainer for 10 minutes for all the water to drain out.

2. To cut carrot, cut it lengthwise into thin slices. Cut each slice diagonally into 2-3" pieces.

3. Again boil 2 cups water with 1 tsp salt. Add thin, diagonal slices of carrots, baby corns and french beans. When the boil returns after a minute, remove from fire. Strain immediately and refresh by adding cold water. Leave the blanched vegetables in the strainer for 15 minutes for the water to drain out completely.

4. Mix all the ingredients of the dressing. Transfer noodles to a bowl and pour ½ of the dressing over the boiled noodles. Mix well and chill in the fridge for 30 minutes.

5. Add the leftover dressing, blanched vegetables and spring onions to the noodles Mix well and chill till serving time.

6. At serving time, top with some roasted peanuts.

Veg Satay with Peanut Sauce

Tofu - an important ingredient in Thai cooking is a rich source of proteins for the vegetarians. You can use paneer instead.

Picture on page 40   *Makes 6 Skewers*

100 gm tofu or paneer - cubed to get 1½ " squares
6 baby corns, small sized - put in boiling water for 3 minutes and wipe dry
6 mushrooms - trim stalk and keep whole, 1 green capsicum - cut into 1" cubes
6 cherry tomatoes or 1 large, firm tomato cut into 8 pieces and pulp removed

MARINADE

½ tsp salt, ¼-½ tsp red chilli powder, 2 tsp brown sugar or gur
2 fresh red chillies - seeded and thinly sliced
3 tbsp coconut milk
½ tsp soya sauce, 1" piece of ginger - grated
1 tsp lemon juice, 1 tsp brown or ¾ tsp regular sugar, 2 tsp cornflour
8-10 flakes garlic - crushed to a paste
½ tsp jeera powder (ground cumin), ½ tsp dhania powder

PEANUT SAUCE

¼ cup roasted salted peanuts, 1 onion - chopped
½ tsp salt, ½ tsp red chilli powder
1 tbsp oil, ½-1 tsp sugar, 1 tsp dhania powder
1 tsp jeera powder (cumin powder)
4-6 flakes garlic - crushed, 1 tbsp butter
1½ tsp lemon juice, 1 tsp soya sauce
1 cup ready-made coconut milk

1. Boil 3 cups water in a pan, add babycorn and mushrooms in it. Boil for 2-3 minutes. Remove from fire, strain and refresh in cold water.

Contd...

2. Mix all ingredients of marinade together. Add tofu or paneer, blanched baby corns, mushrooms & tomatoes. Keep covered for ½ hour or till serving time.

3. Thread a mushroom, then a baby corn, then a cherry tomato or regular tomato piece and lastly a paneer piece onto oiled wooden skewers. Leave behind the marinade. Keep aside. Cook in a preheated oven at 180°C/350°F for 6-7 minutes. Baste (pour) with a spoon the remaining marinade on the sticks and cook for another 2-3 minutes.

4. To make peanut sauce, grind peanuts with the salt to a rough powder.

5. Heat 1 tbsp butter in a heavy bottomed small pan or kadhai. Add crushed garlic. Saute till it starts to change colour. Add onion and cook till soft. Reduce heat. Add ½ tsp red chilli powder, dhania powder and jeera powder. Add only ½ cup coconut milk. Boil, stirring. Cook on low heat for 3 minutes, stirring constantly.

6. Add crushed peanuts, ½ tsp sugar, 1½ tsp lemon juice, 1 tsp Soya sauce and remaining ½ cup coconut milk. Boil. Simmer gently for 5 minutes, stirring occasionally to prevent it from sticking to the pan. Check taste for salt, sugar and lemon juice. Serve sauce with satay.

Toasted Chilli Cashews

Serves 6

125 gms cashewnuts (kaju)
¼ tsp finely chopped garlic
1 dry red chilli - crushed
2 small fresh green chillies - remove seeds and chop finely
1 spring onion - finely chopped uptill the greens, (keep greens separate)
salt to taste

1. Heat a kadhai on fire. Add cashews and roast till it just starts to change colour. Remove from fire.
2. In another wok/kadhai, heat 1 tbsp oil, reduce heat. Add garlic, white of spring onion, dry red chilli, and green chillies, fry till garlic turns golden brown.
3. Add the roasted cashews and the spring onion greens. Mix well.
4. Add salt to taste. Remove from fire. Serve warm.

Spring Rolls

Picture on page 30   *Serves 4*

WRAPPER
1 cup plain flour (maida), ½ cup cornflour
1 tsp salt, 1 tbsp oil, 1 cup water, oil for frying

FILLING
¾ cup seviyaan (vermicelli, Bambino), 1 tbsp soya sauce
¼ cup basil leaves - shredded (use coriander if basil is unavailable)
1 tbsp soya sauce, ½ tsp crushed garlic, ¼ tsp red chilli flakes or powder
½ tsp sugar, ¼ tsp salt to taste, 1 tbsp oil
2 tbsp crushed peanuts (moongphali)

1. To prepare the wrappers, sift plain flour, cornflour and salt. Add oil and water gradually, mixing to make a dough. Keep aside for ½ hour.

2. Makes small balls from the dough. Roll into thin rotis (rounds). Heat a tawa and put one thinly rolled roti on it. Cook on both sides for 2-3 seconds.

Keep rotis covered in a moist cloth in a box.

3. To boil seviyaan, boil 4- 5 cups of water. Add 1 tsp salt and 1 tbsp oil and vermicelli. Let it boil for 2 minutes. Remove from fire. Let it be in hot water for 2 minutes. Strain and refresh with cold water. Leave in the strainer for 5 minutes.

4. To make filling, heat 1 tbsp oil and add garlic.

5. Add seviyaan, soya sauce, basil, red chilli powder or flakes, sugar and salt. Mix well. Add crushed peanuts, mix well.

6. To assemble the wrapper, spread a roti on a flat surface. Cut 1" from all sides to get a square piece.

7. Spread some filling thinly on the upper portion.

8. Fold in ½" from the right and left sides.

9. Holding on, fold the top part to cover the filling. Roll on to get a rectangular parcel; making sure that all the filling is enclosed.

10. Seal edges with cornflour or maida paste, made by dissolving 1 tsp of cornflour or maida in 1 tsp of

Contd...

water. If you chill the rolls for ½ hour, it keeps better shape.

11. Repeat for the remaining rotis and filling. Cover all with a plastic wrap/ cling film and keep aside till serving time.

12. Heat some oil in a large frying pan. Reduce heat and put the rolls, folded side down first in oil. Cook on both sides until crisp and golden. Drain on absorbent paper. Serve with sweet and sour dip given below.

Sweet and Sour Dip

Combine this sweet and tangy dip with any deep-fried Thai starter.

Makes ½ cup (approx.)

a lemon sized ball of imli (tamarind), ½ cup gur, ½ tsp lemon juice
½ tsp salt, ¼ tsp red chilli powder

1. Boil ¼ cup water and imli in a pan. Give one boil. Remove from fire.
2. Strain through a sieve (channi), mashing with the back of a spoon to get pulp.
3. In another pan put 1 tbsp of imli pulp, gur, salt, red chilli powder and ¼ cup water. Give one boil. Remove from fire. Add lemon juice. Chill and serve.

Thai Peanut Corn Cakes

Makes 6-8 corn cakes (kebabs)

¾ cup corn kernels (fresh, tinned or frozen)
¾ cup roasted peanuts (moongphali)
1½ tbsp soya sauce
2 tbsp shredded basil, juice of ½ lemon
1 tbsp ready-made Thai chilli dip (fun food) or ½ tsp sugar
½ tsp red chilli powder, ½ tsp salt, or to taste
4 tbsp cornflour, ½ tsp baking powder

1. Grind corn, peanuts, soya sauce, basil, lemon juice, Thai chilli dip or sugar, red chilli powder, salt, cornflour and baking powder in the mixer to a rough paste.

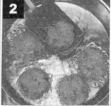

2. Shape into small 1" round kebabs (cutlets). Heat oil in a kadhai and deep fry till golden brown. Serve with hot and sweet dip on page 55.

¥ ¥ ¥ ¥ ¥ ¥
¥
¥
¥
¥

Golden Money Bags

*Small balls of dough rolled into small rounds, filled with a filling and given a
shape to form a money pouch. Starter with an impressive look.*

Gives 15 pouches

POUCHES
1 cup maida (plain flour)
½ cup suji (semolina)
a pinch of soda-bi-carb (mitha soda)
½ tsp salt
1 tbsp oil & oil for frying

FILLING
1 tsp crushed garlic
2 tbsp carrots - grated
2 boiled potatoes - mashed roughly
1 tsp soya sauce
½ tsp salt, ¼ tsp pepper, ½ tsp sugar
2 tbsp roasted peanuts (moongphali)- pounded/crushed
1 tbsp chopped coriander

1. Heat 1 tbsp oil. Reduce heat and add the crushed garlic. Stir for a few seconds.
2. Add carrots and mix.
3. Add potatoes, Soya sauce, salt, pepper and sugar. Cook for 2-3 minutes. Add peanuts and coriander. Cool, adjust seasonings to taste & keep aside.
4. Mix all ingredients of the covering and make a dough with warm water (like chappati dough). Keep aside covered for 30 minutes.

5. Make around 15 small balls and roll one at a time into a small round.
6. Put a teaspoon of filling in the centre and pick up the sides and press at the neck to form a money pouch. Tie the neck with a thin blade of lemon grass if you have.

7. Deep fry to a golden brown colour.
8. Serve hot with a spicy tomato sauce (you may mix 2 tbsp tomato ketchup with 1 tsp red chilli sauce).

Crispy Soft Corn

Picture on page 40   *Serves 4*

FILLING

2 cups ready-made cream style sweet corn (1 tin, see note)
½ tsp garlic paste (3- 4 flakes of garlic- crushed)
¼ tsp salt, ¼ tsp pepper, or to taste
2 tbsp cornflour mixed with 4-5 tbsp water

BATTER

½ cup maida or cornflour, ¼ tsp haldi, a pinch of salt, ½ cup cold water

1. Heat 2 tbsp oil in a pan, add garlic paste and stir on medium flame.
2. Add cream style sweet corn, mix.
3. Add salt & pepper. Mix well & cook for 2-3 minutes on medium flame.
4. Add cornflour paste. Cook for 2 minutes. Remove from fire. Check salt. Let it cool.
5. Put the cooled mixture in a small mixer and grind to a smooth paste.
6. Spread the mixture in a flat plate. Keep in the fridge for atleast 2-3 hours to set.

7. Mix all ingredients of the batter in a bowl.
8. Cut the set mixture carefully into 2" square pieces, (approx. 8-10 pieces). Dip each piece in maida batter and deep fry each piece immediately in hot oil till golden. Serve with the dip given below.

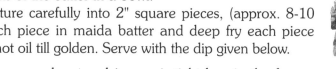

Note: The leftover corn, can be stored in an air tight box in the freezer compartment of the fridge for about 2 months or till further use.

Hot & Sweet Dip

A traditional Thai dip flavoured with crushed red chilli and sugar.

Makes 1½ cups

2 tbsp vinegar, ¾ cup sugar
1 cup water, 1 tbsp red chilli flakes, 1 tbsp salt

1. Combine the vinegar, sugar and water and boil till the mixture becomes a thick syrup.
2. Cool slightly, add the crushed red chillies and the salt.
3. Allow to stand for atleast 6 hours before using. Adjust the vinegar and chillies to your taste.

Vegetable Dim Sums

A steamed snack. Use a steamer basket or an idli stand for steaming them.

Picture on facing page   *Makes 14 pieces*

DOUGH
1 cup maida, 1 tbsp oil, ¼ tsp salt

FILLING
2 tbsp oil, 1 onion - finely chopped
4-5 mushrooms - finely chopped, optional
1 large carrot - grated
2 green chillies - finely chopped, 1 tsp ginger-garlic paste
2 cups grated cabbage (½ small cabbage)
1 tsp salt & ½ tsp pepper powder, or to taste
1 tsp lemon juice

DIPPING SAUCE
4-5 tbsp Soya sauce, 2 tbsp white vinegar, 1-2 tbsp oil
4 flakes garlic - crushed to a paste, ½ tsp chilli powder, ¼ tsp salt
2 tsp tomato ketchup

Contd...

1. For the dough, sift maida with salt. Add oil and knead with enough water to make a stiff dough of rolling consistency, as that for puris.

2. For the filling, heat oil. Add chopped onion. Fry till soft. Add mushrooms and cook further for 2 minutes. Add carrot, green chillies and ginger-garlic paste. Mix well and add the cabbage. Stir fry on high flame for 3 minutes. Add salt, pepper to taste. Add lemon juice and mix well. Remove from fire and keep filling aside.

3. Take out the dough and form small balls. Roll out flat, as thin as possible into small rounds of 2½" diameter.

4. Put some stuffing in the centre and make it into a ball. Roll the ball between the hands to give it an elongated shape like a roll.

5. To steam, put them in idlis stands or a steamer and steam for 10 minutes.

6. Cool the dimsums. Cut a slice from the top to expose the filling. Dot with chilli sauce.

7. For dipping sauce, mix all ingredients in a bowl. Serve with dimsums.

◁ *Stir Fried Mushrooms with Cashewnuts : Recipe on page 78*

Vegetable Curries

About Lemon Grass

Lemon grass : The flavour of lemon grass is similar to that of lemon, yet it has its very own unique taste. To use, discard the bottom 1" of the stalk and peel some of the outer leaves. Chop the stalk and use it in curry pastes. The upper grass like portion is not edible, so it is added to dishes like soups, rice and curries to flavour them but removed from the dish before serving. 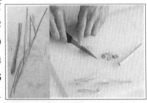 Lemon grass will keep well for about 1-2 weeks in the fridge. Use 1-2 stalks per dish.

Thai Red Curry

Serves 4-6   *Picture on cover*

RED CURRY PASTE

4 Kashmiri red chillies - deseeded & soaked in ½ cup warm water for 10 minutes
½ onion - chopped
8-10 flakes garlic - peeled
½" piece ginger - sliced
1 stalk lemon grass or rind of 1 lemon (see note on page previous page)
1½ tsp coriander seeds (dhania saboot), 1 tsp cumin (jeera)
1 tbsp lemon juice
6 peppercorns (saboot kali mirch), 1 tsp salt

VEGETABLES

100 gms paneer or tofu - cut into 1" square pieces & deep fried till golden brown
6-8 baby corns - slit lengthwise
1 carrot - diagonally sliced
1 small broccoli or ½ cauliflower - cut into small florets (about 8 pieces)

Contd...

5-6 mushrooms - sliced or 8- 10 French beans - cut into 1" pieces
¼ cup chopped bamboo shoots (optional)

OTHER INGREDIENTS

2½ cups thin coconut milk (use readymade coconut milk or for fresh see step 2)
½ tsp soya sauce
15 basil leaves, 5-6 lemon leaves (nimbu ke patte)
1 tbsp oil, salt to taste
1 tsp brown sugar or ½ tsp regular sugar, or to taste

1. Dry roast coriander and cumin seeds on a tawa till they turn light golden and fragrant. Add all the other ingredients of the red curry paste and grind along with the water in which the chillies were soaked, to a very fine paste.

2. Extract coconut milk by soaking 1 grated coconut in 2 cups of warm water. Blend and then strain through a muslin cloth. To the left over coconut and 1 more cup of warm water. Repeat to get 2½-3 cups of milk. You can use ready-made coconut milk also.

3. Heat the oil in a large pan, add the red curry paste and stir fry for 2-3 minutes on low heat.

4. Add 2 tbsp of coconut milk. Add vegetables and cook for 2-3 minutes.
5. Add the rest of the coconut milk, soya sauce and lemon leaves.
6. Simmer on low heat for 5-7 minutes till the vegetables are tender.
7. Add fried paneer or tofu, salt and sugar to taste. Add basil leaves. Boil for 1-2 minutes. Serve hot garnished with red chilli slices with steamed rice or noodles.

Note: You can use any vegetables of your choice.

The red curry paste can be made extra and store in an airtight container (for upto 1 month). Alternatively, freeze for upto 3 months. To obtain a bright red curry paste, use red Kashmiri chillies as for as possible. A little orange red colour may be added if you do not get a bright red curry.

Lemon Rind: In absence of lemon grass, lemon rind makes a good substitute. To get lemon rind, grate a firm, fresh lemon on the finest side of the grater without applying pressure. Grate only the yellow outer skin without grating the white pith beneath it. Rind of 2 lemons would do good for a stalk of lemon grass.

Thai Green Curry

Picture on page 2   *Serves 4*

100 gms tofu or paneer - cut into 1" fingers
½ zucchini - sliced diagonally, ½ small cauliflower - cut into small florets
6 baby corns - halved lengthwise, 1 carrot - diagonally sliced
8- 10 French beans - very diagonally cut into 1" pieces
2½ cups ready-made coconut milk or use ½ cup water with 2 cups coconut
milk if milk is too creamy, 1 tbsp finely chopped lemon grass
1 tsp salt, 3 tsp sugar or gur, ½ -1 tsp soya sauce
3 tbsp chopped fresh basil, 2-3 green or red chillies - slit long for garnishing

GREEN CURRY PASTE
5-6 green chillies - chopped, ½ onion - chopped
1 tbsp chopped garlic, ½" piece ginger - chopped
1 stick lemon grass (use only lower portion) - cut into pieces, discard the leaves
½ tsp salt, ¼ tsp haldi, 15 peppercorns (saboot kali mirch), 1 tbsp lemon juice
1 tbsp coriander seeds (saboot dhania), 1 tsp cumin seeds (jeera)
2-3 lemon leaves (nimbu ke patte) or 1 tsp lemon rind
1 cup fresh basil leaves or ½ cup chopped coriander leaves

1. For the green curry paste, dry roast coriander and cumin seeds for 2 minutes on a tawa till fragrant but not brown. Put all other ingredients of the curry paste and the roasted seeds in a grinder and grind to a fine paste, using a little water.
2. Heat 3 tbsp oil in a kadhai. Add green curry paste. Fry for 2-3 minutes.
3. Add cauliflower. Fry for 3-4 minutes. Add other vegetables and stir for 1 minute. Add 1 cup coconut milk. Stir on low heat for 2-3 minutes.
4. Add chopped lemon grass, salt, sugar and the rest of coconut milk. Boil. Add soya sauce. Cook on low heat for a few minutes or till vegetables are crisp tender.
5. Add basil, tofu or paneer. Give 2-3 boils.
6. Garnish with sliced red or green chillies (long thin slices), basil leaves.
7. Serve hot with boiled/steamed rice.

Note: Discard 1" from the bottom of the lemon grass. Peel a few outer leaves. Chop into small pieces uptil the stem. Discard the upper grass like portion.

Vegetable Yellow Curry

Picture on facing page   *Serves 5*

½ recipe of yellow curry paste (see page 21)
4 tbsp oil
1" piece of ginger - peeled & sliced thinly
2 tbsp roasted peanuts (moongphali) - roughly crushed
1 vegetable seasoning cube (maggi or knorr) - crushed to a powder
1½ cups ready-made coconut milk
1 cup water
5-6 lemon leaves (nimbu ke patte)
1 tbsp finely chopped lemon grass (use only stem, see note given at the end)
15 basil leaves - chopped or coriander leaves
1 tsp brown sugar or regular sugar

VEGETABLES

1 tiny flower of cauliflower or broccoli (200 gms) - cut into small florets
100 gms babycorn - each cut into 2 pieces, lengthwise
¼ cup tinned bamboo shoots (optional)

Contd...

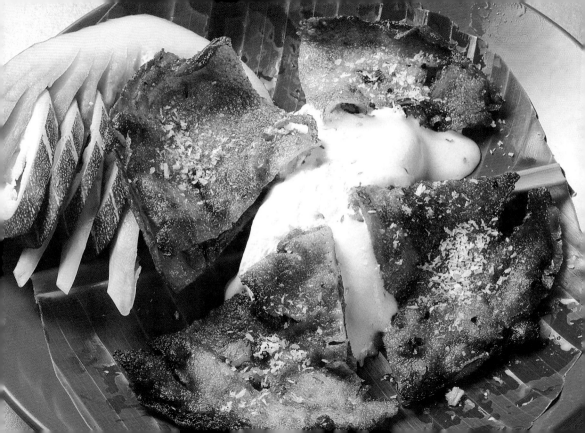

1. Heat 4 tbsp oil in a kadhai. Add yellow curry paste. Fry for 3-4 minutes on low heat.
2. Add ginger, peanuts, seasoning cube and vegetables. Mix well for 2 minutes.
3. Add coconut milk, water, lemon leaves, chopped lemon grass, basil leaves and sugar. Give 3- 4 boils. Serve hot garnished with a red chilli flower or slices with steamed rice or noodles.

 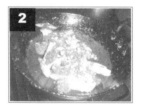 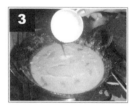

Note: Discard 1" from the bottom of the lemon grass. Peel a few outer leaves. Chop into ½" pieces uptil the stem. Discard the upper grass like portion.

◁ *Date Pancakes : Recipe on page 98*

Masaman Curry

Serves 6

6-7 tbsp masaman curry paste (see page 18)
150 gms babycorn - cut into 1" pieces
250 gms broccoli - cut into medium sized florets (1" pieces)
4 tbsp oil
1 cup thick coconut milk or coconut cream
3½ cups ready-made coconut milk
1 tbsp chopped lemon grass or rind of 1 lemon (see page 11)
1-2 tsp sugar/gur (adjust to taste)
5 tbsp tamarind juice (imli juice)
2 black cardamoms (moti illaichi)
1½" cinnamon stick (dalchini)
1 large onion - cut into 8 pieces & each piece separated to get onion leaves
1½ tsp salt, or to taste
½ tsp haldi powder (optional) - gives a better colour if used
50 gms (½ cup) roasted peanuts (moongphali) - roughly crushed

1. Heat 4 tbsp oil in a kadhai, add masaman curry paste and ½ tsp haldi. Fry for 2 minutes.
2. Add babycorn and broccoli pieces and stir fry for 2-3 minutes.
3. Add coconut milk, chopped lemon grass and upper grass like portion tied into a knot.
4. Except roasted peanuts add all the other ingredients and cook on low heat for 3-4 minutes.
5. Add roasted peanuts. Cook for 2 minutes and serve hot with rice.

Lemon Rind: In the absence of lemon grass, lemon rind makes a good substitute. To get lemon rind, grate a firm, fresh lemon on the finest holes of the grater without applying pressure. Grate only the yellow outer skin without grating the white pith beneath it. Rind of 2 lemons would do good for a stalk of lemon grass.

Bean Curd & Pineapple in Northern Style Curry

Serves 4

250 gms bean curd (tofu) or paneer
½ of a small pineapple - cut into 1" pieces (1 cup)
100 gms bamboo shoots (use tin) - cut into thin slices, optional
3 tbsp oil
¾" piece of ginger - cut into paper thin slices (use only 4-5 slices)
1 lemon sized ball of imli (tamarind) soaked in 1 cup water
1½ cups coconut milk
1½ cups water

PASTE
3 tsp chopped garlic, 3 onions
2 tsp salt, 3 dry red chillies
2 tbsp finely chopped lemon grass, 2 tsp curry powder
1 tbsp soya sauce
1 tbsp brown sugar or regular sugar

1. Grind all the ingredients written under paste to a smooth paste. Use a little water if required.
2. Cut the bean curd (tofu) or paneer into 1" square pieces.
3. Peel the pineapple, remove the eyes and core. Cut into 2" pieces.
4. Boil 1 cup water and add a ball of imli, give 2-3 boils. Strain well through a sieve (channi). Keep strained water aside.
5. Heat oil in wok/kadhai, add sliced ginger, fry for 2-3 minutes.
6. Add prepared paste, cook for 10 minutes.
7. Add imli juice, cook for 2-3 minutes.
8. Add 1½ cups coconut milk and pineapple, give 2 boils.
9. Add 1½ cups water. Boil.
10. Add paneer, mix. Serve hot.

Vegetables in Thick Masala Curry

Serves 4

200 gms mushrooms - cut each into two pieces
200 gms capsicum - cut into ½" slices
1 fresh nariyal (coconut) - grated
4 shredded kaffir lemon leaves (nimbu ke patte), 4 tbsp oil
upper grass portion of 1 lemon grass - tied into a knot (use the edible lower part
in the paste)

CURRY PASTE
1 tbsp grated gur or brown sugar or ½ tbsp regular sugar
4 lemon leaves (nimbu ke patte)
5 large dry red chillies, 1 tbsp soya sauce
5 onions
10 flakes garlic, 1 tsp chopped ginger
2 tbsp chopped lemon grass (see page 10)
1 tsp lemon rind (see page 11)
2 tsp finely chopped coriander
6 peppercorns (saboot kali mirch), 1 tsp salt

1. Grind all ingredients written under curry paste to a smooth paste in a mixer.
2. Grind grated coconut with 2 cups of water in a mixer. Strain the coconut paste through a muslin cloth. Keep coconut milk aside.
3. Cut each mushroom into half.
4. Heat 4 tbsp oil in a wok/kadhai, add the curry paste and fry for 5-6 minutes.
5. Add the mushrooms & cook for 2-3 minutes.
6. Add prepared coconut milk, capsicum, lemon leaves and 1 cup water.
7. Add knotted lemon grass. Give 2 boils. Check salt. Remove from fire. Remove tied lemon grass. Serve hot.

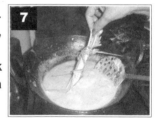

Lotus Stem in Panang Curry

Serves 4

200 gm lotus stem (Bhein) - buy those which are closed at both ends
2 cups milk
1 tbsp finely chopped lemon grass (use only stem, see page 10)
½ cup cream, ½ cup water

BATTER
4 tbsp cornflour
4 tbsp plain flour (maida), ½ tsp salt, ¼ tsp pepper
2 flakes garlic - crushed to a paste
¼ cup water

PANANG CURRY PASTE
1 tsp jeera (cumin seeds), ½ tsp coriander seeds
4 onions - chopped, 8 flakes garlic - chopped
10 dry, red chillies - deseeded. 1 lemon grass - chopped (see page 10)
3 tbsp chopped coriander, 1" piece of ginger - chopped
2 tbsp roasted peanuts, 2 tbsp oil, 2 tsp saunf or 1 star anise (phool chakri)

1. For the paste, dry roast cumin and coriander seeds on low heat on a tawa till they become aromatic and get roasted but not brown, for about 2 minutes.
2. Put all other ingredients of the curry paste and the roasted seeds in a grinder and grind to a fine paste, using a little water if required.
3. Peel lotus stem and cut diagonally into paper thin slices. Wash well.

4. Mix all ingredients of the batter together.
5. Wipe dry the vegetable with a clean kitchen towel. Dip each piece in batter. Deep fry in two batches to a golden yellow colour. Do not brown them. Keep aside.
6. Heat oil in a kadhai, add panang paste, cook for 4-5 minutes.
7. Add milk, chopped lemon grass and water. Give 2-3 boils. Keep aside till serving time.
8. To serve, add cream to the curry and bring to a boil on low heat. Add lotus stem to hot curry, mix. Check salt. Remove from fire. Serve hot.

Note: Panang paste can be stored for 1 week in the fridge.

Crispy Vegetables

Picture on page 103   *Serves 6*

½ of a cauliflower or broccoli - cut into 1" florets
4 large mushrooms - cut each piece into 2 from the middle
8 babycorns - keep whole, 1 tsp garlic paste
½ red, ½ yellow capsicum, ½ green capsicum - cut into 1" square pieces
1 onion - cut into 8 pieces, 20 basil leaves - keep whole, remove stem

BATTER

¼ cup rice flour or ¼ cup raw rice (kachcha chaawal) - ground to a powder in a mixer
1 tbsp chopped lemon grass, ¾ cup cornflour
1 tsp soya sauce, ¾ cup chilled water- approx., 1 tbsp oil
½ tsp red chilli flakes, ¾ tsp salt

PASTE

1 tbsp lemon juice, 1 tbsp oil
4 dry, red chillies, 1 tbsp black bean sauce
3 tbsp ready-made mango chutney
1 tsp soya sauce, 1" stick cinnamon (dalchini)
1 tbsp tomato ketchup, 1 tsp honey, ½ tsp salt

1. Cut all vegetables as written above.
2. Put all ingredients written under paste in a mixer and grind to a paste.
3. Use ready-made riceflour or roughly grind ½ cup rice in a mixer to a powder. Roast this ground rice in a kadhai till it starts to change colour. Sieve the roasted rice to get a fine powder.
4. Mix all ingredients of batter in a bowl. Mix well and add cauliflower, baby corns and mushrooms to the batter and keep aside for 30 minutes or more.
5. Heat oil in a kadhai. Mix the vegetables in the batter well and deep fry till golden brown.
6. At serving time, heat 1 tbsp oil. Add 1 tsp garlic paste and onions. Stir fry for 2 minutes. Add the capsicums. Stir.
7. Add the mango chutney paste. Stir fry for 2 minutes.
8. Add ¼ cup water.
9. Add fried vegetables and basil, mix well and serve.

Orange Glazed Sesame Vegetables

Stir-fried vegetables in a tangy orange sauce with peanuts and sesame seeds.

Picture on facing page   *Serves 4*

½ cup paneer - cut into thin long strips
1 cup broccoli (hari gobhi) or cauliflower - cut into small florets
6 babycorns - sliced diagonally
1 green capsicum - cut into 1" square pieces
1 cup mushrooms - sliced
1 tbsp finely chopped lemon grass (use only stem, see page 10)
2 tbsp soya sauce
1 cup ready-made orange juice (tropicana or real)
1 tsp cornflour
2 tbsp roasted sesame seeds (white til)
2 tbsp peanuts (moongphali)
¾ tsp salt and ½ tsp pepper or to taste
a pinch of sugar, or to taste

1. Roast sesame seeds and peanuts on a hot tawa till golden. Remove from fire and keep aside.
2. Heat 3 tbsp oil in a large pan or wok, add the paneer strips and stir fry till they turn brown. Remove paneer from pan, keep aside.

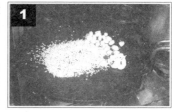

Cutting of all vegetables

3. To the same pan, add the broccoli, babycorn, capsicum, mushrooms and lemon grass. Stir fry for 1 to 2 minutes.
4. Mix soya sauce, orange juice and cornflour in a cup. Stir this mixture into the vegetables. Cook stirring for 4-5

minutes till the sauce has thickened and glaze develops.
5. Add sesame seeds, peanuts, salt, pepper and sugar to taste. Add paneer. Cook for 2 minutes. Serve hot with rice or noodles.

◁ *Dates on Fire : Recipe on page 100*

Noodles 'n' Rice

Thai Flat Noodles

Picture on page 103   *Serves 2*

200 gm flat noodles, preferably rice noodles - break into 4"- 5" length
½ cup shredded basil leaves
1 tsp garlic paste, 4 tbsp crushed peanuts (moongphali)
3 tsp tomato ketchup, ¼ tsp salt or to taste

1. Boil 6-8 cups water. Add noodles to boiling water and stir with a fork. Let noodles be in hot water for 1-2 minutes. Drain. Wash with cold water and strain. Keep in the strainer for 15 minutes for all the water to drain out. Sprinkle 1 tbsp oil and mix.

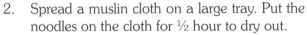

2. Spread a muslin cloth on a large tray. Put the noodles on the cloth for ½ hour to dry out.

3. Heat 4 tbsp oil. Add garlic paste, cook till golden. Add peanuts and basil leaves.
4. Add boiled noodles. Add tomato ketchup and salt.
5. Mix well with the help of 2 forks. Fry for 2-3 minutes. Serve hot.

¥ ¥ ¥ ¥ ¥ ¥
¥
¥
¥
¥

Pad Thai (Flat Noodles with Vegetables)

Serves 4-5

7-8 cups boiled (400 gms) noodles, preferably, flat noodles
2 large carrots - cut into diagonal slices and then into strips of ¼" thickness
1 cup bean sprouts with long shoots - optional
1 stalk lemon grass - very finely chopped
6-8 lemon leaves - shredded
10 -12 garlic flakes - crushed (1½ tbsp)
1 onion - shredded or thinly sliced
2½ tsp salt
½ -1 tsp soya sauce, 6-7 tbsp lemon juice
4 tbsp roasted peanuts - coarsely ground
5 tbsp oil

SUGAR SYRUP
3 tbsp sugar mixed with ¼ cup water and boiled for a minute

RED CHILLI PASTE
4-5 dry red chillies - deseed and ground to a paste with 1 tbsp water

1. Boil 8-10 cups water with 2 tsp salt and 1 tbsp oil. Add noodles to boiling water. Remove from fire. Let noodles be in hot water for 1 minute. Strain. Rinse in cold water. Drain and keep aside. Keep aside in the strainer for all the water to drain out.
2. Prepare sugar syrup and keep aside.
3. Wash sprouts in several changes of water. Leave in the strainer.
4. Heat 5 tbsp oil in a non stick wok or pan. Reduce heat. Add garlic. Stir. Add red chilli paste. Fry for about 1 minute.
5. Add lemon grass, onions and bean sprouts. Fry for 2 minutes till onions turn soft.
6. Add carrots and lemon leaves. Mix. Stir fry for 2 minutes. Reduce heat.
7. Add noodles. Do not mix. Add 2½ tsp salt, sugar syrup, lemon juice, soya sauce and 4 tbsp peanuts. Increase heat and mix well using 2 spoons.
8. Serve hot sprinkled with some roasted and crushed peanuts.

Sticky Rice

Sticky rice is easier to eat with chopsticks! It's a little sweet because of the honey added to it. Use new rice because the grains stick to each other on cooking.

Serves 6

1½ cups uncooked rice (short grained new rice)
2 tbsp oil, 1 onion - sliced
2 flakes garlic - crushed
2 spring onions - chop white and green part separately
2 green chillies - chopped
½ cup peas (matar)
½ tsp jeera powder (cumin powder), ½ tsp dhania powder (ground coriander)
1 tsp saunf (fennel seeds) - crushed
1 tsp salt, ½ tsp pepper

MIX TOGETHER
3 cups veg stock or 3 cups of water mixed with 1 vegetable seasoning cube (maggi or knorr)
2 tbsp honey, 2 tbsp soya sauce

1. Wash and soak rice. Keep aside.
2. Mix all the ingredients written under mix together in a bowl. Keep aside.
3. Heat oil in a large deep pan, add sliced onion and garlic and stir-fry for 4-5 minutes or until onion is soft.

4. Add white part of spring onion, green chillies and peas.
5. Add jeera powder, dhania powder, crushed saunf, salt and pepper. Stir-fry for 1 minute.
6. Drain rice and add to the pan. Stir for 3-4 minutes on low heat.
7. Add stock-honey mixture and green of spring onion. Stir and bring to a boil.

8. Reduce heat and cook covered for 10 minutes or until rice is done and the water gets absorbed. Serve hot.

Tip: Do not use old rice. The newer the rice, the more sticky it becomes when cooked. To see if the rice is old or new, shake the packet of rice. If powder stick to the sides, it is old rice.

¥ ¥ ¥ ¥ ¥ ¥
¥
¥
¥
¥

Masaman Curried Rice

Delicious aromatic rice which can be had plain without any other dish. It is a complete meal by itself almost like a masala vegetable biryani.

Picture on cover   *Serves 4-5*

1 cup basmati rice (soaked for 10-15 minutes)
Masaman paste (given on page 22)
½ cup french beans - diced
½ cup carrots - diced, ½ capsicum - diced
2 tsp coconut powder (maggi) mixed with ½ cup milk
2 tsp salt, ½ tsp haldi powder
2 stalks lemon grass - tie into a knot, discard when rice is ready
3 tbsp lemon juice, 4 tbsp oil
1 cup coconut milk OR use half packet coconut powder (maggi)
mixed with ½ cup milk

1. Heat oil in a kadhai or a saucepan (patila) with a well fitted lid. Add masaman curry paste. Fry till aromatic and leaves oil.
2. Mix 2 tsp coconut powder with ½ cup milk.
3. Add this coconut milk, in the kadhai, cook till nearly dry.
4. Add vegetables, stir fry for a minute.
5. Add salt, haldi, lemon juice, lemon grass, 1 cup coconut milk, 1 cup water and soaked rice.
6. Give one boil. Cook covered for 5-8 minutes or till all the water has dried and the rice is cooked. Discard lemon grass.
7. Serve hot garnished with fresh coriander, lemon wedges and tomato slices.

¥ ¥ ¥ ¥ ¥ ¥
¥
¥
¥
¥

Glass Noodles with Sesame Paste

Glass noodles are thin long translucent noodles. In the absence of these the regular noodles or rice seviyaan can be used.

Serves 6

100 gms glass noodles or rice seviyaan
2 tbsp oil
3 spring onions - cut into rings, till the greens, keep white separate

SESAME PASTE (GRIND ALL TOGETHER)
3 tbsp sesame seeds (til) - soak for 10 minutes in 5 tbsp hot milk and 2 tbsp
water and then grind to a paste
½ tsp red chilli powder or to taste, ¾ tsp salt
4 flakes garlic - finely chopped
1½ tbsp soya sauce
½ tsp sugar

1. Cut white spring onion into rings till the greens.
2. In a large pan, boil 8 cups water with 1 tsp salt and 1 tsp oil. Remove from fire. Add noodles to hot water. Cover & keep aside for 5 minutes in hot water. Drain.

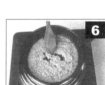

3. Wash with cold water several times. Strain. Leave them in the strainer for 15-20 minutes, turning them upside down, once after about 10 minutes to ensure complete drying. Apply 1 tsp oil on the noodles and spread on a large tray. Dry the noodles under a fan for 15-20 minutes. Keep aside till further use.
4. Grind all ingredients of sesame paste to a smooth paste.
5. Heat oil in a pan, remove from fire. Swirl the pan to coat the bottom of the pan nicely with oil. Add white portion of spring onions, stir for a minute.

6. Add prepared sesame paste mixture, mix well and stir for 2 minutes on low heat.
7. Add boiled noodles, mix well. Add spring onion greens. Mix & remove from fire.

Desserts

Date Pancakes

Picture on page 68   *Serves 8*

½ cup cornflour, ½ cup plain flour (maida)
¼ cup milk or slightly more
2 tsp melted butter
2 tbsp powdered sugar

FILLING

300 gm dates (khajoor) - deseeded and finely chopped (2 cups)
2 tbsp sesame seeds (til) - toasted on a tawa (griddle) till golden
2 tbsp butter, ½ cup water

TO SERVE

vanilla ice-cream
some desiccated coconut (coconut powder)

1. Sift the cornflour and plain flour together. Add butter and sugar. Add just enough milk and knead to a firm, smooth dough. Cover and keep aside for 15 minutes.
2. For the filling, toast sesame seeds in a non stick pan or a tawa till golden. Remove from pan and keep aside. In the same pan melt butter. Add dates and stir for 2 minutes. Add water and cook on low heat for about 2-3 minutes, till a little pulpy and slightly dry. Remove from fire and mix in the toasted sesame seeds. Keep filling aside.
3. Make 8 small balls from the dough. Roll out each ball to a thin chappati.
4. Spread some filling on half of it. Dot the edges with water all around. Fold over to get a semi circle. Press the edges to stick together. Make all pancakes in the same way and keep covered with a cling wrap till serving time.
5. To serve heat a cup of oil in a frying pan and gently slide the stuffed pancake. Shallow fry on medium heat until crisp, turning sides. Cut into two pieces and top with desiccated coconut. Serve with vanilla ice cream.

Dates on Fire

Steamed date cakes prepared in a pressure cooker flambed on the serving table. You can make this cake in the oven also. See note given below.

Picture on page 86   *Serves 4*

½ cup deseeded & chopped dates, ¼ cup water, ¼ tsp soda-bi-carb (mitha soda)
50 gm (¼ cup) white butter, ½ cup brown sugar
¼ cup maida, ¼ cup cornflour, 1 tsp baking powder, 1 egg, 1 tbsp milk

MIXED SPICE CRUSH TOGETHER
1" stick cinnamon (dalchini), 2 cloves (laung)

TO FLAMBE (OPTIONAL)
some desiccated coconut, 3 tbsp rum or brandy sauce

1. Soak finely chopped dates in ¼ cup water in a bowl. Sprinkle ¼ tsp soda on them. Mix well and keep aside for 15 minutes.
2. Grind dates to a puree a keep aside.
3. Beat butter with brown sugar till fluffy. Add the date paste to butter sugar mixture.
4. Sift maida, cornflour and baking powder.

5. Beat egg lightly. Add maida mixture and egg to the date mixture.
6. Add the mixed spice and beat well.
7. Add 1 tbsp milk to get a soft dropping consisting. Beat well.
8. Grease 4 small steel katoris a cake moulds. Pour cake mixture in them.
9. Take a pressure cooker. Put ½" high water in it. Place the "jaali" or the perforated steel plate of the cooker in it. (No water in the cooker !) Place the katoris on the jaali. Close the cooker. Remove the weight of the cooker. Place cooker on fire. After 2 minutes reduce heat to minimum. (It is better to put a tawa on low heat and then place the cooker on the tawa. This reduces the heat further). Keep cooker on fire on 30 minutes. Remove from fire. Open the cooker after 5-7 minutes.

10. At serving time put the cakes on a platter sprinkle some desiccated coconut.
11. If you want to flambe cake then take 1-2 tbsp rum or brandy in a kadahi and heat it on fire. After 2 minutes, when it catches fire, pour immediately on the cakes. Serve immediately with flames on the cake.

Note: You can bake the cake at 180° C for 20 minutes in a preheated oven.

Coconut Custard

Serves 8

2¼ cups coconut milk
7 tbsp sugar or to taste
4 tbsp cornflour dissolved in ½ cup water
1½ tsp cinnamon powder (dalchini powder)
a drop of green colour

1. Heat coconut milk and sugar in a saucepan to a boil.
2. Add cornflour paste and cook, stirring till it starts to thicken and coats the back of a spoon. Add colour. Mix well. Remove from fire immediately.
3. Add cinnamon powder. Serve.

Crispy Vegetables : Recipe on page 80 ➢
Thai Flat Noodles : Recipe on page 88 ➢

Nita Mehta's BEST SELLERS (Vegetarian)

All Time Favourite SNACKS

SANDWICHES

Taste of RAJASTHAN

Desserts Puddings

ZERO OIL

Delicious Parlour ICE-CREAMS

Indian Cooking HANDI TAWA KADHAI

Different ways with CHAAWAL

PASTA & CORN

PARTY FOOD

PANEER all the way

MENUS from around the world